by Ken MacNeil

79 Main Street, Newtongrange,
Midlothian EH22 4NA
Tel: 0131 344 0414 Fax: 0845 075 6085
E-mail: info@lang-syne.co.uk
www.langsyneshop.co.uk

Design by Dorothy Meikle
Printed by Ricoh Print Scotland

ISBN 978-1-85217-077-6

SEPT NAMES INCLUDE:

MacGougan
MacGrail
MacNeal
MacNeill
MacNelly
Neal
Neale
Neil
Neilson
Nelson
Nielson

MacNeil

MOTTO:
To Conquer or Die.

CREST:
On a red and ermine
baronial chapeau a rock.

TERRITORY:
Outer Hebrides.

Chapter one:

The origins of the clan system

by Rennie McOwan

The original Scottish clans of the Highlands and the great families of the Lowlands and Borders were gatherings of families, relatives, allies and neighbours for mutual protection against rivals or invaders.

Scotland experienced invasion from the Vikings, the Romans and English armies from the south. The Norman invasion of what is now England also had an influence on land-holding in Scotland. Some of these invaders stayed on and in time became 'Scottish'.

The word clan derives from the Gaelic language term 'clann', meaning children, and it was first used many centuries ago as communities were formed around tribal lands in glens and mountain fastnesses.

The format of clans changed over the centuries, but at its best the chief and his family held the land on behalf of all, like trustees, and the ordinary clansmen and women believed they had a blood relationship with the founder of their clan.

There were two way duties and obligations. An inadequate chief could be deposed and replaced by someone of greater ability.

Clan people had an immense pride in race. Their relationship with the chief was like adult children to a father and they had a real dignity.

The concept of clanship is very old and a more feudal notion of authority gradually crept in.

Pictland, for instance, was divided into seven principalities ruled by feudal leaders who were the strongest and most charismatic leaders of their particular groups.

By the sixth century the 'British' kingdoms of Strathclyde, Lothian and Celtic Dalriada (Argyll) had emerged and Scotland, as one nation, began to take shape in the time of King Kenneth MacAlpin.

Some chiefs claimed descent from

ancient kings which may not have been accurate in every case.

By the twelfth and thirteenth centuries the clans and families were more strongly brought under the central control of Scottish monarchs.

Lands were awarded and administered more and more under royal favour, yet the power of the area clan chiefs was still very great.

The long wars to ensure Scotland's independence against the expansionist ideas of English monarchs extended the influence of some clans and reduced the lands of others.

Those who supported Scotland's greatest king, Robert the Bruce, were awarded the territories of the families who had opposed his claim to the Scottish throne.

In the Scottish Borders country – the notorious Debatable Lands – the great families built up a ferocious reputation for providing warlike men accustomed to raiding into England and occasionally fighting one another.

Chiefs had the power to dispense justice and to confiscate lands and clan warfare produced a society where martial virtues – courage, hardiness, tenacity – were greatly admired.

Gradually the relationship between the clans and the Crown became strained as Scottish monarchs became more orientated to life in the Lowlands and, on occasion, towards England.

The Highland clans spoke a different language, Gaelic, whereas the language of Lowland Scotland and the court was Scots and in more modern times, English.

Highlanders dressed differently, had different customs, and their wild mountain land sometimes seemed almost foreign to people living in the Lowlands.

It must be emphasised that Gaelic culture was very rich and story-telling, poetry, piping, the clarsach (harp) and other music all flourished and were greatly respected.

Highland culture was different from other parts of Scotland but it was not inferior or less sophisticated.

Central Government, whether in London or Edinburgh, sometimes saw the Gaelic clans as

"The spirit of the clan means much to thousands of people"

a challenge to their authority and some sent expeditions into the Highlands and west to crush the power of the Lords of the Isles.

Nevertheless, when the eighteenth century Jacobite Risings came along the cause of the Stuarts was mainly supported by Highland clans.

The word Jacobite comes from the Latin for James – Jacobus. The Jacobites wanted to restore the exiled Stuarts to the throne of Britain.

The monarchies of Scotland and England became one in 1603 when King James VI of Scotland (1st of England) gained the English throne after Queen Elizabeth died.

The Union of Parliaments of Scotland and England, the Treaty of Union, took place in 1707.

Some Highland clans, of course, and Lowland families opposed the Jacobites and supported the incoming Hanoverians.

After the Jacobite cause finally went down at Culloden in 1746 a kind of ethnic cleansing took place. The power of the chiefs was curtailed. Tartan and the pipes were banned in law.

Many emigrated, some because they

wanted to, some because they were evicted by force. In addition, many Highlanders left for the cities of the south to seek work.

Many of the clan lands became home to sheep and deer shooting estates.

But the warlike traditions of the clans and the great Lowland and Border families lived on, with their descendants fighting bravely for freedom in two world wars.

Remember the men from whence you came, says the Gaelic proverb, and to that could be added the role of many heroic women.

The spirit of the clan, of having roots, whether Highland or Lowland, means much to thousands of people.

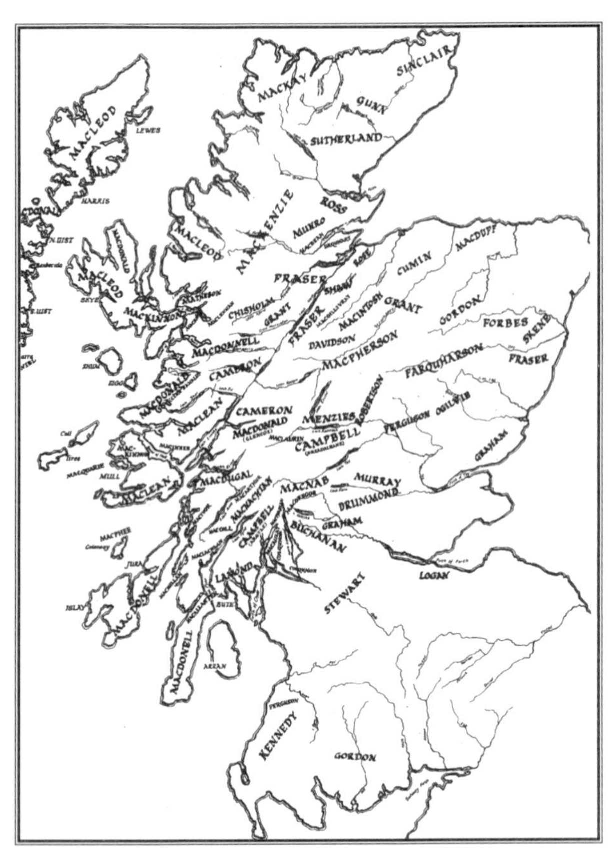

A map of the clans' homelands

Chapter two:

Marriage and slaughter

The MacNeils can trace their origins through the O'Neil's of Ireland to the ancient Egyptians. According to popular tradition the first Neil married an Egyptian princess who rescued Moses from the Nile and her son, Gaidhall or Gall, moved to settle in Spain, then Ireland.

Many of the Gaels who entered Ireland and eventually established a high Kingship at Tara came from the East by the way of the Iberian Peninsula. At first the Irish O'Neil's held only the title Prince of Ulster but eventually they made the high kingship hereditary in their line. According to the legend they were crowned at Tara, on the Stone of Destiny – Jacob's pillow when he saw the angels going up and down the ladder to heaven. This later became the Stone of Scone, used at the coronation of all the kings of Scotland and Britain since the Middle Ages, and returned to Scotland in the winter of 1996.

The legends surrounding the O'Neil's are many. Neil of the showers called for God's help in a famine and was given in turn a shower of gold, a shower of honey and eventually, what he had requested, a shower of wheat.

These O'Neil's were based in Antrim when the race now known as the Scots began to cross to Argyll and the isles in the fifth century, bringing Christianity to the land to which they eventually gave their name.

It is at this point that the controversies concerning the descent of the MacNeils of Scotland begin. Clan oral tradition asserts that the son of Hugh the Solitary, an Ulster O'Neil, is said to have come to Barra in the 11th Century and to have been the founder of the MacNeils of Barra. Non Clan sources suggest the MacNeil name was formed by Gaelic families on the mainland who acquired Barra in the 14th Century.

Perhaps the truth lies in the traditional Highland saying that the MacNeils had a boat of their own at the flood. They are certainly one of the oldest Gaelic families, if not the oldest.

The Norseman invaded Scotland and made a complete conquest of the Western Isles. Some Scholars believe that all the place names in the Hebrides are of Norse origin though it seems likely that many are Gaelic names with Norse admissions.

Barra for example is probably derived from the seventh century Irish St Barr who became the patron of the MacNeils with the Norse ending ay being added at some later date to form barray, the Isle of St Barr.

The history of the isles and the MacNeils shows a continual intermingling of the Norse and Celtic cultures. And although the threat of direct Norwegian rule was broken forever at the battle of Largs in 1266 the semi-independence of the West persisted in north Celtic Lordship of the Isles.

It is generally agreed that the MacNeils acquired Barra by marriage though when this happened is matter of dispute.

Ruary MacNeil mentioned in a document of 1409 is the first named MacNeil in the ruling line.

A daughter of the last Norse leader fell in love with an illegitimate son of the MacNeils then betrayed her father. She brought her lover over to slay the Norseman and his bodyguards as they lay asleep in their great hall. Clan legend says MacNeil walked up both sides of the room decapitating the Norseman one by one. The Norse chief was the last to be killed and his head was thrown with two others into a well which is still called the well of heads.

Thus the MacNeils solved the Norse problem by the usual joint method of marriage and slaughter. Eventually the lordship of the Isles passed to the MacDonald's with whom the MacNeils were long closely allied. In 1427 Gillian MacNeil received a charter for Barra from Alexander MacDonald of the Isles.

In the 1470's another MacNeil fought with the Lord of the isles against his rebellious son Angus Og at the Battle of Bloody Bay, off

Ardnamurchan point, though he quickly made his peace with the Crown when James the Fourth decided to suppress the Lordship in 1493.

But this MacNeil and his successors were not well disposed to meekly obeying the rule of law and order and hankered after the old Western independence. The Black Galley of the Norsemen and the Lord of the Isles now became a symbol of piracy and disruption in the eyes of the Scottish Kings.

As late as 1591 MacNeils went on full scale pirate raids against the Burkes on the West Coast of Ireland and even later, in1675, the King's messenger attempted to serve a summons for piracy on the chief at his base, Kisimul. Stones and gunshots were fired so the messenger was in danger of being brained as he tried to a fix the writ to the castle doors. As he made his escape the chief's younger brother sallied forth from the fortress and chased him to a neighbouring island where the writ was ripped to shreds and thrown to the four winds.

Chapter three:

Battles and dungeons

The MacNeils had a long and stormy relationship with the monarchs of Scotland. All Scottish Clans were in the main loyal to the crown with a tradition of quarrelsome disobedience when any attempt was made to interfere with their independence. Because of their remote situation the MacNeils were more troublesome.

In the 16th Century it became the custom of the chiefs to send a herald on to the walls of Kisimul each evening after dinner to proclaim to the sea and wind.

Hear all you people and listen o ye nation – the great MacNeil of Barra having taken his meal...

A MacNeil chief and his clansmen set out to loot a Spanish galleon which had been driven ashore off Barra. As they were dismantling the ship some of the men began to wonder whether Spain might decide to take revenge for their actions.

That, responded the chief with awesome dignity, was something for the King of Spain and MacNeil of Barra to settle between themselves. The MacNeil chiefs certainly had a high and mighty opinion of themselves!

In fact the MacNeils did not regard the Kings of Scotland as a natural overlord until quite late in the day. In 1545, for example, the chief tried to arrange an alliance against the Scottish crown with Henry the eight of England and rode to London as if the Scots were foreigners. This spirit of treasonable autonomy culminated in the reign of Ruary the turbulent, chief at the time of King James VI.

His most famous exploit was the capture and looting of two ships of Queen Elizabeth the First of England returning from the Indies. The Queen sent a strong protest to King James at Edinburgh and felt obliged to take action. Roderick Mackenzie of Kintail was given the formidable task of taking the MacNeil in his lair.

Rather than use outright force he disguised himself as a Flemish merchant trading in wines and arrived at Kisimul with armed men in one hold and many casks of drink in the other.

Ruary was enticed on board by the offering of a night's free sampling and ended up beneath the table after an astonishing display of drinking. When he woke up the next morning he found that the ship as well as his head was swaying and that Mackenzie had already begun the long journey from the north back to Edinburgh.

King James, expecting to find a savage desperado, was impressed by Ruary's good breeding and manners. Quizzed about the looting of Elizabeth's ship Ruary said he had done it in revenge over the execution of Mary Queen of Scots.

So instead of being sent to the gallows Ruary was given a nominal fine and released to go home with a warning about his future conduct. Mackenzie of Kintail, for his part, was awarded the general Lordship of Barra and the surrounding isles. It appears, however that Mackenzie had occasion to chastise Ruary again at a later date and mounted a full-scale siege on Kisimul Castle. Ruary was trapped inside with only a few followers and very little provisions and sat down in desperation to try and work out some way to get rid of his enemy who were content to wait and starve them out.

Finally he remembered about a pile of sheepskins kept in one of the outhouses as winter bedding and decided to try and trick Mackenzie into believing that flock of sheep was kept inside the castle.

But how could the skins be made to look as if they were new? The castle dogs gave him the answer. They were slaughtered and their blood was smeared over the sheepskins which were then thrown over the castle wall, as if to dry.

When Mackenzie saw them he told his men the siege was futile as MacNeil obviously had enough meat to last for six months. And with that the invaders sailed away!

On another occasion Ruary had great difficulty sailing up the North Channel on his way home from a raid on the Isle of Man. When he finally reached Castle Bay, in which Kisimul island stands, he was unable to land at the fortress because night had fallen so he camped on the mainland of Barra.

Since Kisimul is only a short distance from the shore the campfire was clearly visible from the castle walls and the boatman was put in a terrible quandary. His orders were to fire on any such encampment but he knew that MacNeil was expected back at any moment and might have been driven ashore by the stormy conditions. He decided to solve the problem by loading the castle cannon with the insides of a bullock so that he could always say he had fired on the camp. The shot was deadly accurate landing on the campfire and the MacNeils found themselves supplied with a delicious and already cooked meat supper.

Ruary had two sons – one was born legitimately by a daughter of the Duart MacLean's, the other out of wedlock by the sister of MacDonald of Clanranald. Inevitably the two sons fought each other for the succession even before their father's death.

Ruary himself favoured the Macdonald line and the legitimate heirs were packed off to Mull to plot with their MacLean In-laws. Eventually the MacLean sons decided to recover their rights by storming Kisimul, which they did successfully.

Ruary died in the castle dungeons, still a prisoner of his MacLean sons, and was forced to give them the succession, the MacDonald claimants being bought off with land in South Uist.

Feuds of this sort were common throughout the highlands in the 16th Century and, in the West, continued with vigour until the 1745 rebellion as no new MacNeil chief was accepted by the clan until he had made at least one raid on his neighbours. As one quarrel blew over another sprang up. Generally the MacNeils veered between their old allies the MacDonald's and the MacLean's of Duart who, like the Campbell's, had risen in influence on the fall of the Lordship of the Isles.

In 1585, for the only time in history, the MacNeils were split in battle when the mainland MacNeils fought with the Macdonald against their Barra cousins who turned out for the

MacLean's. The MacLean side won, killing 340 of the enemy, and in the process incurred the wrath of the King. James the sixth then issued a series of writs against the Western Clans and successfully contained their quarrels, though it was almost impossible to enforce the law effectively on an island as remote as Barra.

In 1601 there was another fight with the Macdonalds which resulted in the MacNeils losing most of their South Uist possessions. Then Neil of MacNeil, a son of Ruary Tartar, fought with almost all the surrounding clans during his chieftainship.

The MacNeils supported the Stewart line during the Jacobite uprisings. Their first appearance in the royal cause was as part of the army which tried to restore Charles the second after his father's execution, and which was routed at the battle of Worcester in 1651.

In 1688 the MacNeil chief received a new charter for his Barra lands from James the seventh and repaid the debt by fighting in Bonnie Dundee's army at Killiecrankie. It was here that he was seen panting and groaning under the weight of a huge battleaxe in a furious downhill charge which scattered the army. The MacNeils also fought at Sheriffmuir in 1715 and the Chief's sons were forced to go into exile when the Stewart cause went down again.

The Clan's contribution to the '45 was less glorious but even more costly. Bonnie Prince Charlie made his first landing on Scottish soil in MacNeil territory at Esriskay. Roderick the Dove, Chief of MacNeil, was no great warrior as his name suggests and preferred to contribute to the cause by sending secret supplies of men and money to join the Prince's army as it marched south.

After the uprising ended in the fiasco at Culloden Roderick was arrested and taken to London along with Flora Macdonald, Lord Lovat and many others, where he was kept prisoner for three years. Roderick had been accused of giving one of Prince's lieutenant's gold from a Spanish galleon which had come into Mac Neil's possession.

Chapter four:

Plunder and ruin

As we have seen the MacNeils came to Barra from Knapdale on the mainland and those who remained in Argyll were still the senior line as late as 1530 when Torphin O'Neil of Gigha was referred to by the Privy Council as chief and principal of the entire clan and the surname of the MacNeils. The main line failed shortly afterwards however and though a cadet line later established itself on Colonsay they were dominated by the Campbells to such an extent that the chieftainship of the clan passed conclusively to the MacNeil of Barra.

The last notable MacNeil of this line was John of Oronsay. A great land reformer of the mid-19th century, he incurred the opposition of his tenants by trying to replace their middle of the floor peat fires with wall chimneys. They insisted the fires had to stay where they were so the wee folk, or fairies, could continue to dance round them.

The Barra MacNeils too are famous for their tales of magic and second sight and when the Irish priests who brought the island back to Catholicism landed in 1651 they reported that the Barra men were superstitious rather than heretical. Islanders were great believers in mermaids whose appearance always foretold disaster for those who saw one. A popular tale tells of a six man fishing crew who saw a mermaid popping in and out of the water as they returned to shore. They took this as a clear sign not to attempt a landing and despite their exhaustion and the wind blowing them strongly ashore they set themselves to go away to another island.

They finally succeeded after struggling all night with the elements and when they next went out to sea were rewarded with a bumper catch of fish.

The story telling traditions and natural beauty of Barra have attracted visitors there for many centuries. A visitor in 1549 described it as a fruitful isle abounding in fish. Within the south west of the isle there is a castle pertaining to MacNeil of Barra. The date of the castle's origins is as much disputed as the date of MacNeils arrival on Barra. What we do know for certain is that by the 15th century it was considered virtually impregnable and this, with the isolation of Barra, made for a uniquely close relationship between clan and chief.

In 1645 a visitor reported that when a tenant's wife dies he addresses himself to MacNeil, representing his loss and at the same time desires that he should be pleased if the chief would recommend a wife to him so that he can continue to manage his affairs. MacNeil then seeks out a suitable match which takes place almost immediately.

These strong ties lasted until Culloden after which the chief's military power was broken and with it the main foundation of clan allegiance.

All these were swept away by the anti clan legislation of the 1750s and by the end of the 18th century the chiefs had moved out of Kisimul

Castle and had become little better known than lowland lairds.

The final disaster came in 1838 when the kilt industry failed and the last chief of the old line, General Roderick MacNeil, was forced to sell the estate to Gordon of Cluny.

Under this family the immigration which had begun after Culloden accelerated and by 1850 there were thousands of MacNeils who had made their home in Canada. By this time Kisimul castle was a plundered ruin, the very stones of its walls removed to provide ballast for empty ships returning to the mainland.

The late 19th century was a low point for the clan and Barra. Several factors enabled both to survive. Firstly, the chieftainship passed into the hands of an American family whose fourth member, Robert Lister MacNeil, decided in 1915 to take up his chiefly rights in Scotland and attempt to rebuild Kisimul Castle as a home for his line. After a lifetime's effort this work was virtually completed at the time of his death in 1970.

Today the clan has a restored home in its

traditional stronghold. The other main factor in the continued life of the clan is the extraordinary cohesion of the MacNeils themselves both in Scotland and America. In part this results in their religious traditions, in part from their way of life as crofters and fishermen but in the main it comes from their determination to retain their family identity whatever the circumstances.

In Canada, for example, an almost exact replica of the Hebridean community grew up at Cape Breton island in the Gulf of St. Lawrence. The MacNeil love of independence of spirit, colourful characters and, above all, great story-telling survived the crossing of the Atlantic.

Today Kisimul, Barra and the MacNeil clan are all in better condition than at any time in the last 200 years and it appears that the four strands of history portrayed in the chief's arms – Gaelic tradition, Highland independence, royal service and family loyalties, will continue into another century.

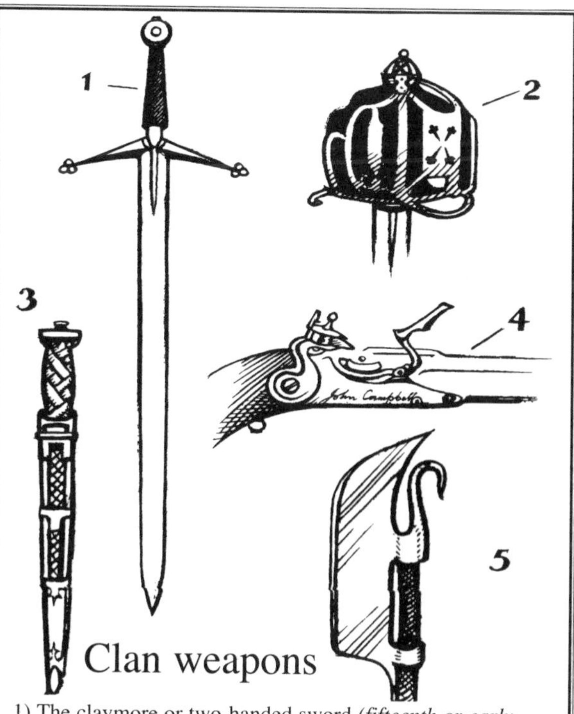

Clan weapons

1) The claymore or two-handed sword *(fifteenth or early sixteenth century)*
2) Basket hilt of broadsword made in Stirling, 1716
3) Highland dirk *(eighteenth century)*
4) Steel pistol *(detail)* made in Doune
5) Head of Lochaber Axe as carried in the '45 and earlier